I1030435

Food Dudes

HENRI NESTLÉ

Food Company Creator

Heather C. Hudak

Checkerboard
Library

An Imprint of Abdo Publishing
www.abdopublishing.com

abdopublishing.com

Published by Abdo Publishing, a division of ABDO, PO Box 398166, Minneapolis, Minnesota 55439. Copyright © 2018 by Abdo Consulting Group, Inc. International copyrights reserved in all countries. No part of this book may be reproduced in any form without written permission from the publisher. Checkerboard Library™ is a trademark and logo of Abdo Publishing.

Printed in the United States of America, North Mankato, Minnesota
062017
092017

THIS BOOK CONTAINS
RECYCLED MATERIALS

Production: Mighty Media, Inc.
Editor: Rebecca Felix
Cover Photographs: Nestlé Historical Archives, Vevey (inset); Shutterstock (main)
Interior Photographs: AP Images, p. 27; iStockphoto, p. 18; Library of Congress, p. 9; Nestlé Historical Archives, Vevey, pp. 1, 13, 19, 21, 23, 25; Shutterstock, pp. 7, 11, 16; Wikimedia Commons, pp. 5, 17; Wisconsin Historical Society, WHS-28607, p. 15

Publisher's Cataloging-in-Publication Data

Names: Hudak, Heather C., 1975-, author.
Title: Henri Nestlé: food company creator / by Heather C. Hudak.
Other titles: Food company creator
Description: Minneapolis, MN : Abdo Publishing, 2018. | Series: Food dudes |
    Includes bibliographical references and index.
Identifiers: LCCN 2016962532 | ISBN 9781532110832 (lib. bdg.) |
    ISBN 9781680788686 (ebook)
Subjects: LCSH: Nestlé, Henri, 1814--1890--Juvenile literature. | Nestlé (Firm)--
    United States--Biography--Juvenile literature. | Businesspeople--United States-
    -Biography--Juvenile literature.
Classification: DDC 641.6 [B]--dc23
LC record available at http://lccn.loc.gov/2016962532

Contents

Early Life. 4

Science Studies. 6

Business Owner 8

Business Goes Flat 10

A Concrete Plan 12

Baby Blues. 14

Milk Man. 16

Cereal Boom 18

New Owners 20

Nestlé Company. 22

Milk & Chocolate. 24

Nestlé Today 26

Timeline 28

All about Labels 29

Glossary 30

Websites 31

Index. 32

Early Life

Do you have a sweet tooth? Then you have probably enjoyed Nestlé sweets! From Crunch and Butterfinger candy bars to chocolate chips, Nestlé is the brand behind some of the world's favorite sweet treats.

Today, the Nestlé company also produces coffee, ice cream, pet food, and more. The road to becoming one of the best-known food manufacturers was a long one. The brand now found in supermarkets all over the world got its start in a European town.

Heinrich Nestle was born on August 10, 1814, in Frankfurt am Main, Germany. Heinrich's father, Johann, came from a family of **glaziers**. Johann took on the family business of glass fitting in Töngesgasse, Germany. He married Anna Maria Catharina Ehemann. She also came from a family of glaziers.

Heinrich was the eleventh of fourteen children. By the time of his birth, five of his brothers and sisters had died of diseases, such as whooping cough and measles. It was not uncommon for babies to die young in those days. This would become a topic of study for Heinrich in later years.

Heinrich's birthplace, Frankfurt am Main, is Germany's fifth-largest city.

Science Studies

Shortly after his Heinrich's birth, Johann gave up the family business. He began making window glass and glass bottles. He made extra money working as an agent for the Paris General **Insurance** Company.

Not much is known about Heinrich's schooling as a boy. It is known that he continued his studies past his teenage years. By age 20, Heinrich had completed a four-year **apprenticeship** in **pharmacy**. During this time, he studied several subjects, including Latin and **chemistry**.

Heinrich finished his studies. Like most pharmacy apprentices, he then become a journeyman. This meant he traveled to other places to learn more about the trade.

As a journeyman, Heinrich left Germany and moved to Switzerland. There, he worked for a pharmacist named Marc Nicollier. Nicollier had a pharmacy in the town of Vevey.

As he settled in to French-speaking Switzerland, Heinrich wanted to fit in. He changed his name to Henri, which sounded more French than Heinrich. He also added an accent to his last name, Nestlé.

Schools didn't have science labs until the late 1800s. When Heinrich was a student, science studies included reading textbooks and memorizing information instead of performing experiments.

Business Owner

Nestlé worked under Nicollier for several years. He learned much about running a **pharmacy**. By 1839, Nestlé qualified as a pharmacist's assistant. This meant he could now do his own chemical experiments. He could also sell medicines.

Nestlé wanted to open his own business in Vevey. He asked Nicollier to help him get started. Nicollier arranged for Nestlé to buy a property his brother was selling.

At first, Nestlé didn't have the money to purchase the property. But in 1843, he was able to borrow it from a wealthy aunt. Nestlé's brother Wilhelm also moved to Switzerland. Wilhelm helped Nestlé run his new business from 1844 to 1857.

Nestlé wanted to start making his own products, such as mineral water and lemonade. But he was eager to repay his aunt the money he had borrowed. So, he started out by making the same products Nicollier's brother had, since the property was set up for it.

Nestlé made and sold oils, fertilizers, and more. As he earned money from sales, Nestlé was able to expand his product line. He then also began making mineral water and **carbonated** lemonade. Nestlé's **carbonated** lemonade was the first to be made in Switzerland. Soon, Nestlé began selling flavored sodas and alcoholic spirits to local inns. He became known as an **entrepreneur**.

The business property Nestlé bought was on the shore of Lake Geneva in Vevey.

Business Goes Flat

Nestlé's business was very successful throughout the 1840s. But by the 1850s, he wanted to expand his offerings. He began looking for new business ventures.

As a child, Nestlé had been fascinated by the introduction of gas lighting in Frankfurt. Gas lighting was the process of combining liquid gases to produce artificial light and heat. It was used in streetlamps and homes.

In the mid-1800s, many small towns did not yet have gas lighting. It was too costly to build the pipes that transported the gas. Nestlé developed a liquid gas that was not transported by pipes. At first, Vevey was not interested in Nestlé's gas. But by 1858, the town used it to power 12 streetlamps.

Around the same time, Nestlé took on a business partner. Wilhelm had left for another job. And Nestlé needed someone to help finance his business. He partnered with Guillaume Keppel, a business owner who had taken over Nicollier's **pharmacy**. Keppel continued to run his own pharmacy. But he also became a partner in Nestlé's business. However, Nestlé continued to run the company.

Gas lighting was used in large cities in the early 1800s. Its use became widespread later that century.

By the late 1850s, Nestlé had stopped making most of his other products to focus mainly on making liquid gas. But in 1863, Vevey got a gasworks plant. Nestlé's liquid gas was no longer needed. Once again, he changed directions with his business.

A Concrete Plan

As Nestlé grew his business, his family also expanded. While visiting Frankfurt in 1860, he married Anna Clémentine Therese Ehemant. She went by her middle name, Clémentine. The two would remain married the rest of Nestlé's life.

In 1861, Nestlé's life changed again. He found himself in need of a new business partner. Keppel did not have as much money as Nestlé had thought to help fund Nestlé's business. The two men parted ways. Two weeks later, Nestlé formed a partnership with a man named Louis Auguste Bérengier.

Bérengier would fund Nestlé's business for the next six years. Nestlé bought new machinery with the money Bérengier brought to the business. Nestlé continued making fertilizer and liquid gas. He also built a machine to cut licorice candy into sticks.

Nestlé was earning a decent living. But he wanted to create something new. He began experimenting with new product lines. He decided to focus on the construction industry.

In 1866, Nestlé was still in business with Bérengier. But he also went into business with François Monnerat that year. Monnerat

Nestlé was an innovator. He adapted his products to benefit his customers.

owned a business making plaster and lime for building materials. Together, the men planned to make cement and concrete blocks.

However, within a year, Monnerat pulled out of the project. Nestlé's business contract with Bérengier also ended in 1867. But Nestlé already had bigger plans in mind.

Baby Blues

Nestlé's ideas had led him to explore many branches of business and make a wide variety of products. This included fertilizers, liquid gas, concrete, and more. In the late 1800s, his ideas took him in another direction. He wanted to create a **nutritious** substitute for breast milk that could be fed to infants.

At the time, many babies were not getting the nutrients they needed. Breast milk provided the best nutrients for new babies. But some women could not breastfeed. Instead, their babies were often fed porridge, animal milk, or a mixture of milk and flour.

These substitutes for breast milk were hard to **digest**. They caused many stomach problems. Poor nutrition was responsible for many infant deaths in Europe until the late 1800s. Approximately 15 to 25 percent of babies did not live to see their first birthdays.

Infant illness and deaths troubled Nestlé, as several of his own brothers and sisters had died young. He began to research a new, nutritious substitute for breast milk. The results of his studies spurred the start of the Nestlé food and beverage empire.

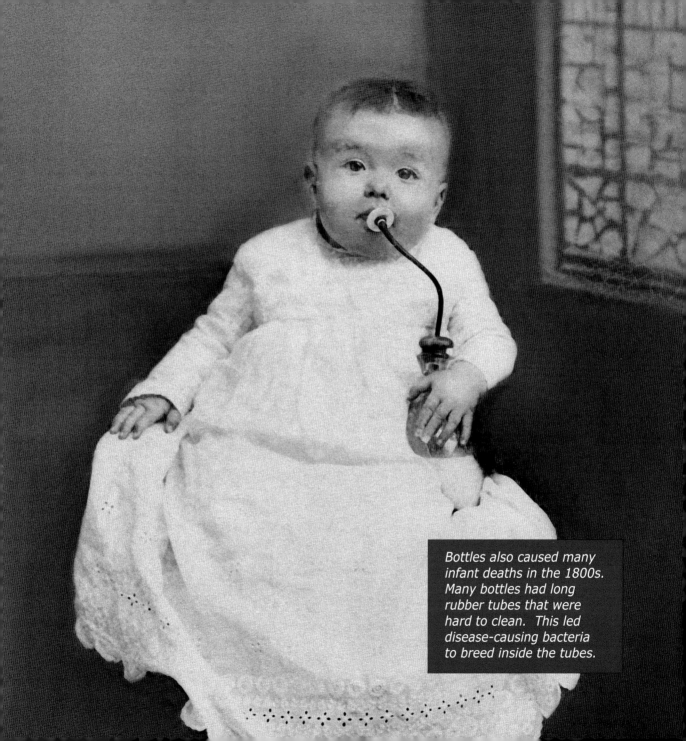

Bottles also caused many infant deaths in the 1800s. Many bottles had long rubber tubes that were hard to clean. This led disease-causing bacteria to breed inside the tubes.

Milk Man

Nestlé was determined to do something about the high rate of infant deaths. He knew pure cow's milk was one of the best substitutes for a mother's milk. Nestlé **condensed** cow's milk but added ground biscuit and **bicarbonate** to make it easier to **digest**.

In Switzerland, cow's milk was easy to come by. But it was less available in other parts of Europe. Nestlé needed to find a way to preserve the milk so he could ship it to other countries. He tested several different forms and mixtures. Finally, Nestlé came up with a **nutrient**-rich, powdered-milk **cereal**.

Nestlé healing a baby known as "Little Wanner" proved the value of his creation. Little Wanner could not keep down any food. He was very ill. In October 1867, Nestlé fed the baby the milk cereal. After a few days, Little Wanner's health improved. People said it was a miracle.

Word quickly spread about Little Wanner's recovery. Nestlé's cereal became an overnight success. The cereal was known as *Farine Lactée*, or "flour with milk." It was **nutrient** rich and it tasted good. It was the first of its kind.

Mothers from Vevey and the surrounding area began buying Farine Lactée. They used it as a substitute for their breast milk. Doctors also gave their approval of the **cereal**.

By November, Nestlé focused on his new product. He spent less time on his other products. He stopped working on the concrete project altogether.

A vacuum sugar apparatus in 1851. Nestlé used a similar machine to preserve milk through a process called vacuum evaporation.

Cereal Boom

As word spread about Farine Lactée, people all over the world wanted to get their hands on it. Nestlé needed to make more **cereal**, and quickly. He borrowed money from his mother-in-law. Nestlé used this money to order machines that allowed him to **mass-produce** his milk cereal.

Nestlé worked long hours to fill the growing demand for Farine Lactée. He continued to make small improvements to the recipe as he did so. Nestlé had his cereal tested often. He wanted to be sure it was the best it could be. In 1872, he earned a gold medal for his work at an exhibition in Paris, France. Nestlé's cereal had helped reduce infant deaths due to poor **nutrition**.

Farine Lactée had been proven scientifically successful. But Nestlé had more to do to grow his business. He had to advertise his cereal to mothers, who were his main customers.

Nestlé's name was a big part of his marketing. It appeared in every product and advertisement he created.

Nestlé knew mothers saw Farine Lactée as more than just a **cereal**. They believed it could also help keep their babies from becoming ill. So, Nestlé decided not to sell the cereal at grocery stores with other food. Instead, he would to sell it at **pharmacies**.

Nestlé relied on mail advertisements and **word of mouth** to promote his product. He also wrote newspaper articles and letters about his product. By 1874, Nestlé had sold 1.6 million cartons of his cereal, in 18 countries.

New Owners

Sales of Nestlé's milk **cereal** were good. Nestlé used profits he made to pay back money he had borrowed or to grow the business. Nestlé also had many business dealings across Europe and North America. It was difficult for him to keep up. Nestlé wanted help running the business, but he couldn't find a partner he trusted.

Although he did not have a partner, Nestlé did have help making Farine Lactée. By 1874, approximately 30 people worked for him in Vevey. Nestlé began assigning some of his workload to them.

Nestlé stepped away from the business but kept up his scientific research. Word spread that he was winding down his career. Many people wanted to buy Nestlé's business. So, he decided to sell.

Pierre-Samuel Roussy was Nestlé's flour supplier and friend. Roussy joined with his nephew, Gustave Marquis, and Nestlé's former partner Monnerat to make Nestlé an offer.

The men gave Nestlé 1 million French francs, two horses, and a carriage in exchange for his company. The sale was made on March 1, 1875. The new business was called Farine Lactée Henri Nestlé.

Nestlé headquarters have remained in Vevey since the company began.

Nestlé Company

The new owners of Farine Lactée Henri Nestlé wasted no time expanding the business. Within a year, they doubled the amount of milk **cereal** being made. But the company soon faced a new obstacle. The Anglo-Swiss **Condensed** Milk Company launched its own powdered-milk cereal, creating major competition.

Anglo-Swiss was owned by American brothers who moved to Switzerland in the 1860s. The company mainly made condensed milk. In 1877, it began selling powdered-milk cereal as well. Many people realized it was easier to buy their condensed milk and cereal from the same supplier. Farine Lactée sales began to drop.

In an effort to increase profits, the Nestlé company started making condensed milk in 1878. The plan was a success. Customers could then buy both their condensed milk and milk cereal from either supplier. Profits rose at the Nestlé company.

Although he no longer owned the company, Nestlé was still interested in its success. He supported the company's products. When it began making condensed milk, Nestlé gave some to his friend Daniel Peter. Peter had used Anglo-Swiss condensed milk as

Farine Lactée Henri Nestlé continued to grow. By 1890, the company employed 470 people!

an ingredient to make chocolate. He began using Nestlé **condensed** milk as well. Over the next several years, the Nestlé's milk chocolate Peter made would become very well-known and popular.

Nestlé died of a heart attack on July 7, 1890. He was 76 years old. His name and memory lived on at Nestlé company, even as the company expanded.

Milk & Chocolate

By 1904, the Nestlé company began selling chocolate made by Peter and Kohler Swiss General Chocolate Company. It continued to sell **condensed** milk and milk **cereal** as well. Anglo-Swiss was still a major competitor in this market. In 1905, the competitors solved this problem. The companies **merged** to become the Nestlé and Anglo-Swiss Condensed Milk Company.

The merged company was very successful. It began with a combined 20 factories, but this number soon increased. Over the next few years, Nestlé and Anglo-Swiss factories expanded to every continent but Antarctica.

There was a big demand for both condensed milk and chocolate during **World War I**. The British army gave condensed milk to soldiers. This was because the milk was easy to carry and could last a long time.

Crisis struck when demand for condensed milk lessened after the war. The **Great Depression** was in effect as well, which caused sales to drop. Nestlé and Anglo-Swiss began developing ideas for new products.

In 1929, Nestlé and Anglo-Swiss **merged** with Swiss chocolate company Peter, Cailler, Kohler, Chocolats Suisses S.A. Its chocolate brand, Cailler, became an important product line for the company. From there, the company continued to expand its food product line each year. In 1938, it launched Nescafé. The instant coffee quickly became one of most popular brands in the company's history.

Cailler is one of Switzerland's most well-known chocolate brands.

Nestlé Today

In the 1940s, the Nestlé and Anglo-Swiss **Condensed** Milk Company **merged** with a Swiss company called Alimentana S.A. It was known for making soups and seasonings. The new company became known as Nestlé Alimentana.

Nestlé Alimentana developed many new products. In 1948, it introduced a powdered iced tea called Nestea, and Nesquik, a chocolate powder used to flavor milk. By 1957, the company sold canned foods as well, such as Maggi ravioli.

Throughout the 1960s and 1970s, Nestlé Alimentana bought several other food companies. In 1974, the company branched out in a new direction when it bought **shares** in the beauty manufacturer L'Oréal. In 1977, Nestlé Alimentana was renamed Nestlé S.A.

Nestlé S.A. continued buying companies and developing new products in the 1980s. It bought Carnation, a US brand known for its evaporated milk, in 1985. The 1990s and 2000s saw even more companies become part of Nestlé S.A. Today, Nestlé is the largest food and beverage company in the world. It has more than 2,000 brands under its label.

Paul Bulcke was the CEO of Nestlé from 2008 to 2016.

Nestlé S.A. continues to carry out research on **nutrition**, which was so important to Henri Nestlé. In 2011, it established Nestlé Health Science and the Nestlé Institute of Health Sciences. These branches research science-based nutrition that can help prevent and treat medical conditions. The Nestlé company helps people make informed choices about the foods they eat. And with its thousands of products, it's very likely their choices include something Nestlé!

Timeline

1814	Heinrich Nestlé was born on August 10 in Frankfurt am Main, Germany.
1839	Nestlé qualified as a pharmacist's assistant in Switzerland.
1843	Nestlé bought a business property in Vevey, Switzerland.
1858	Vevey used Nestlé's liquid gas to power 12 streetlamps.
1860	Nestlé married Anna Clémentine Therese Ehemant.
1860s	Nestlé began experimenting with infant nutrition.
1867	Nestlé used his milk cereal to heal Little Wanner, and it soon became known as a miracle food.
1874	Nestlé's milk cereal, Farine Lactée, had sold more than 1.6 million cartons worldwide.
1875	Nestlé sold his company on March 1.
1890	Henri Nestlé died of a heart attack on July 7.

All about Labels

When Henri Nestlé sold his company, he also sold his own name. It was on all of his product labels. But his name was not the only thing on Nestlé labels. These are some of the other types of information on Nestlé packages.

Nest Trademark

Nestlé wanted a special mark to help his product stand out. He came up with an image of a bird's nest, as *nestlé* means "little nest" in Swiss German. Nestlé first began using the trademark in 1868. Today, a version of the nest trademark still appears on many Nestlé labels.

Seal of Approval

Nestlé wanted a way to show people his milk cereal was scientifically approved. He made a deal with a French chemist named J.A. Barral. For part of the 1860s, every tin of cereal had Barral's name and a seal of approval. In 1872, Nestlé began using his own name as a seal of approval on his products.

Glossary

apprenticeship - an arrangement in which a person learns a trade or a craft from a skilled worker.

bicarbonate - a chemical compound made up of carbon, oxygen, and hydrogen.

carbonated - combined or infused with carbon dioxide.

cereal - a grain-based breakfast food often eaten with milk.

chemistry - a science that focuses on substances and the changes they go through.

condensed - changed to a more compact or dense form.

digest - to break down food so the body can absorb it.

entrepreneur - one who organizes, manages, and accepts the risks of a business or an enterprise.

glazier - someone who installs glass in window frames.

Great Depression - the period from 1929 to 1942 of worldwide economic trouble. There was little buying or selling, and many people could not find work.

insurance - a contract that helps people financially if they are sick or hurt.

mass-produce - to make in large quantities, usually using machines.

merge - to combine or blend, such as when two or more companies combine into one business.

nutrient - a substance found in food and used in the body. Nutrition promotes growth, maintenance, and repair. Something that does this is nutritious.

pharmacy - a store in which drugs are made and sold. A pharmacist is a person licensed to prepare and sell drugs.

share - one of the equal parts into which the ownership of a company is divided.

word of mouth - informal communication.

World War I - from 1914 to 1918, fought in Europe. Great Britain, France, Russia, the United States, and their allies were on one side. Germany, Austria-Hungary, and their allies were on the other side.

Websites

To learn more about Food Dudes, visit **abdobooklinks.com**. These links are routinely monitored and updated to provide the most current information available.

Index

A
Alimentana S.A. 26
Anglo-Swiss Condensed
   Milk Company 22, 24

B
Bérengier, Louis Auguste
   12, 13
birth 4

C
chocolate 4, 23, 24,
   25, 26
concrete 13, 14, 17
condensed milk 16, 22,
   23, 24, 26

D
death 23

E
education 6, 8
Ehemann, Anna Maria
   Catharina 4
Ehemant, Anna
   Clémentine Therese 12

F
family 4, 6, 8, 10, 12, 14,
   18

Farine Lactée 17, 18, 19,
   20, 22
Farine Lactée Henri
   Nestlé 20, 22

G
Germany 4, 6, 10, 12
Great Depression 24

I
infant nutrition 14, 16,
   17, 18, 19

K
Keppel, Guillaume 10,
   12
Kohler Swiss General
   Chocolate Company
   24

L
liquid gas 10, 11, 12, 14
Little Wanner 16

M
Marquis, Gustave 20, 22
milk cereal 16, 17, 18,
   19, 20, 22, 24
Monnerat, François 12,
   13, 20, 22

N
Nestle, Johann 4, 6
Nestle, Wilhelm 8, 10
Nestlé Alimentana 26
Nestlé and Anglo-Swiss
   Condensed Milk
   Company 24, 25, 26
Nestlé S.A. 26, 27
Nicollier, Marc 6, 8, 10

P
Peter, Cailler, Kohler,
   Chocolats Suisses S.A.
   25
Peter, Daniel 22, 23,
   24, 25
pharmacies 6, 8, 10,
   19, 26

R
Roussy, Pierre-Samuel
   20, 22

S
Switzerland 6, 8, 9, 10,
   11, 17, 20, 26

W
World War I 24